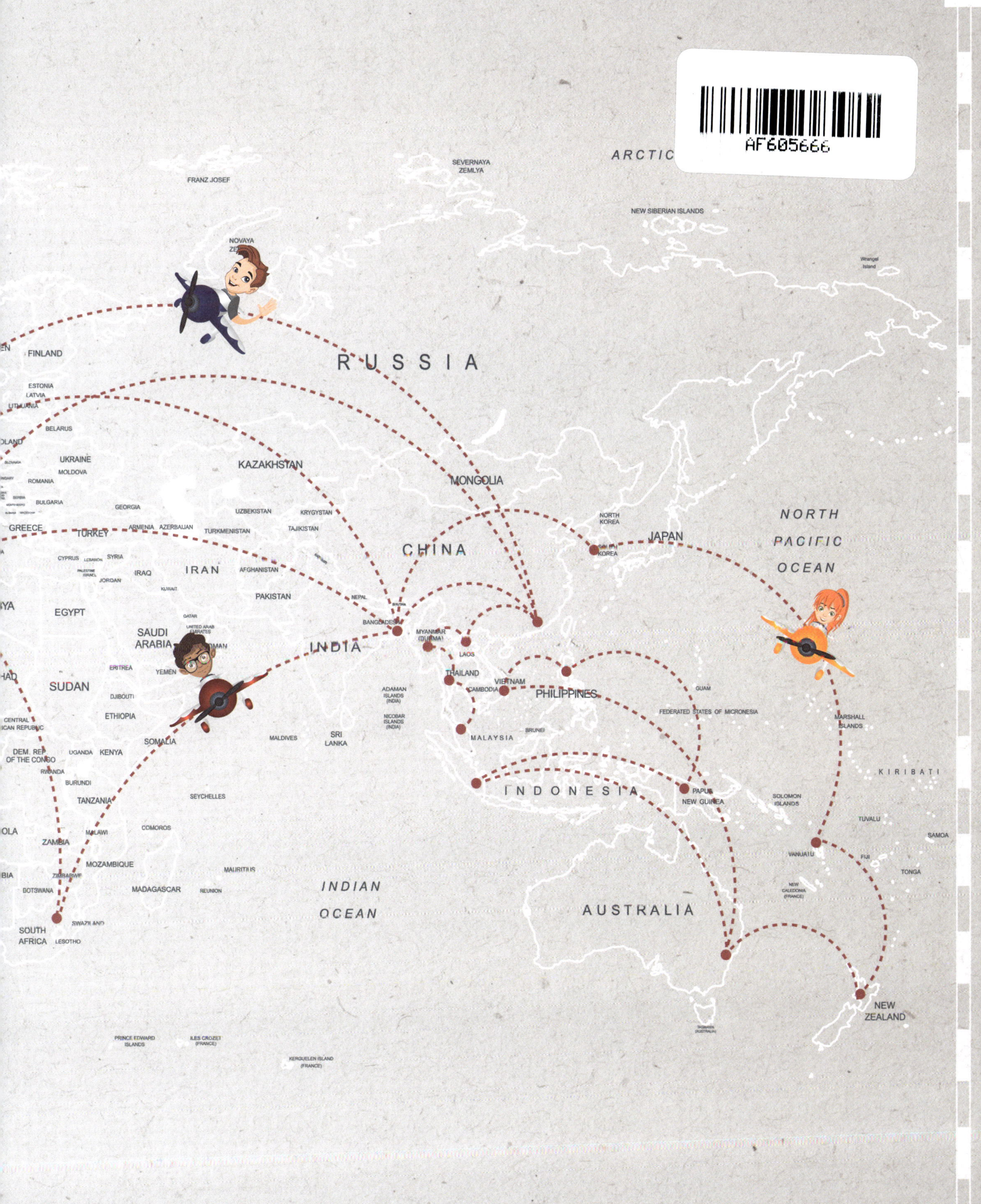
ARCTIC
SEVERNAYA ZEMLYA
FRANZ JOSEF
NEW SIBERIAN ISLANDS
Wrangel Island
FINLAND
RUSSIA
ESTONIA
LATVIA
LITHUANIA
BELARUS
UKRAINE
MOLDOVA
ROMANIA
BULGARIA
KAZAKHSTAN
MONGOLIA
GEORGIA
UZBEKISTAN
KRYGYSTAN
TAJIKISTAN
GREECE
TURKEY
ARMENIA
AZERBAIJAN
TURKMENISTAN
NORTH KOREA
JAPAN
NORTH PACIFIC OCEAN
CHINA
SOUTH KOREA
CYPRUS
SYRIA
IRAQ
JORDAN
IRAN
AFGHANISTAN
KUWAIT
PAKISTAN
NEPAL
EGYPT
QATAR
UNITED ARAB EMIRATES
BANGLADESH
SAUDI ARABIA
OMAN
INDIA
MYANMAR (BURMA)
LAOS
ERITREA
YEMEN
THAILAND
VIETNAM
SUDAN
DJIBOUTI
ADAMAN ISLANDS (INDIA)
CAMBODIA
PHILIPPINES
GUAM
ETHIOPIA
NICOBAR ISLANDS (INDIA)
FEDERATED STATES OF MICRONESIA
CENTRAL AFRICAN REPUBLIC
MALDIVES
SRI LANKA
BRUNEI
MARSHALL ISLANDS
SOMALIA
MALAYSIA
DEM. REP. OF THE CONGO
UGANDA
KENYA
KIRIBATI
RWANDA
BURUNDI
INDONESIA
PAPUA NEW GUINEA
SOLOMON ISLANDS
TANZANIA
SEYCHELLES
TUVALU
ZAMBIA
MALAWI
COMOROS
SAMOA
VANUATU
FIJI
MOZAMBIQUE
MAURITIUS
TONGA
ZIMBABWE
NEW CALEDONIA (FRANCE)
BOTSWANA
MADAGASCAR
REUNION
INDIAN OCEAN
AUSTRALIA
SOUTH AFRICA
SWAZILAND
LESOTHO
NEW ZEALAND
PRINCE EDWARD ISLANDS
ILES CROZET (FRANCE)
KERGUELEN ISLAND (FRANCE)

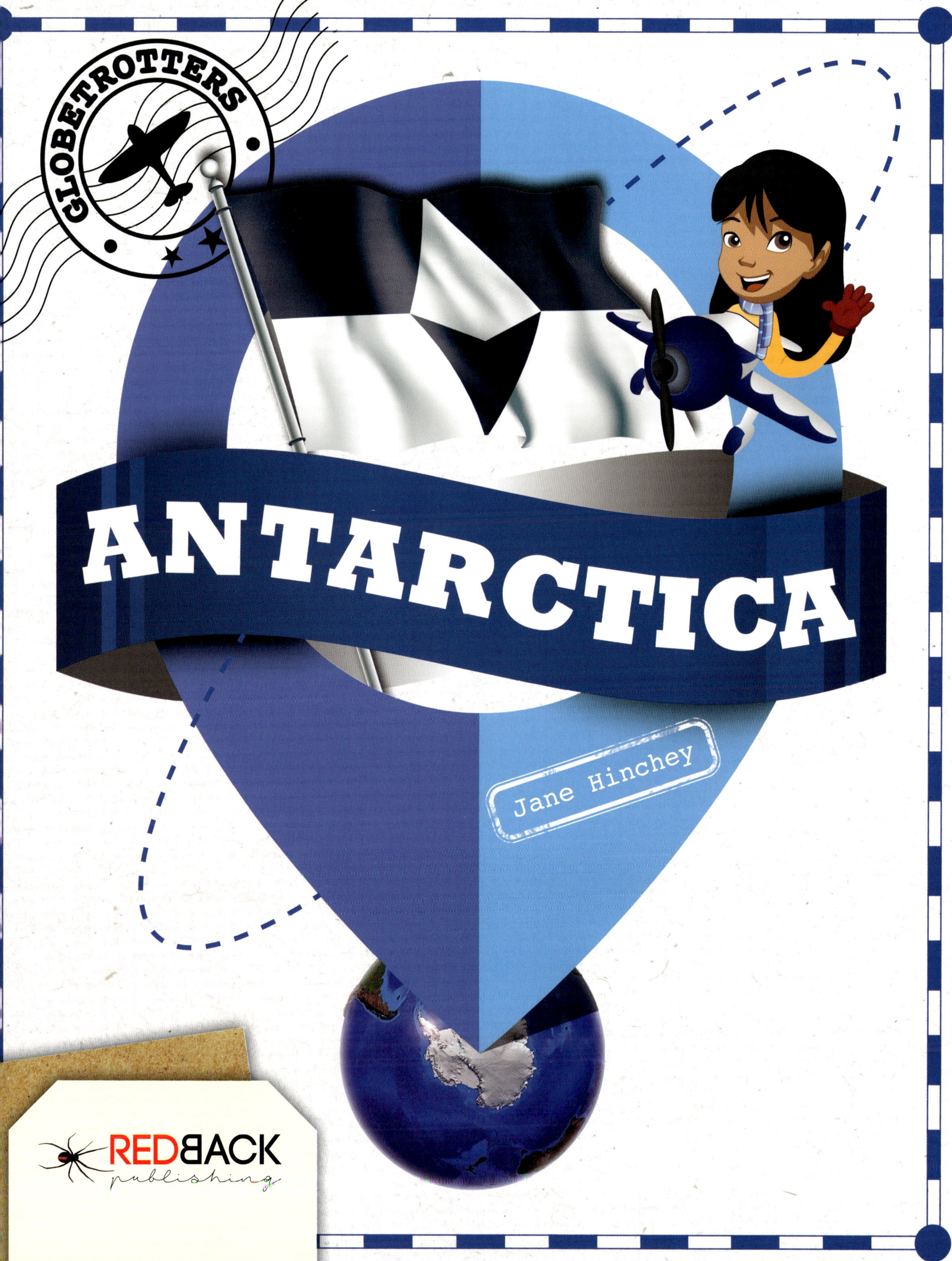
GLOBETROTTERS
ANTARCTICA
Jane Hinchey
REDBACK
publishing

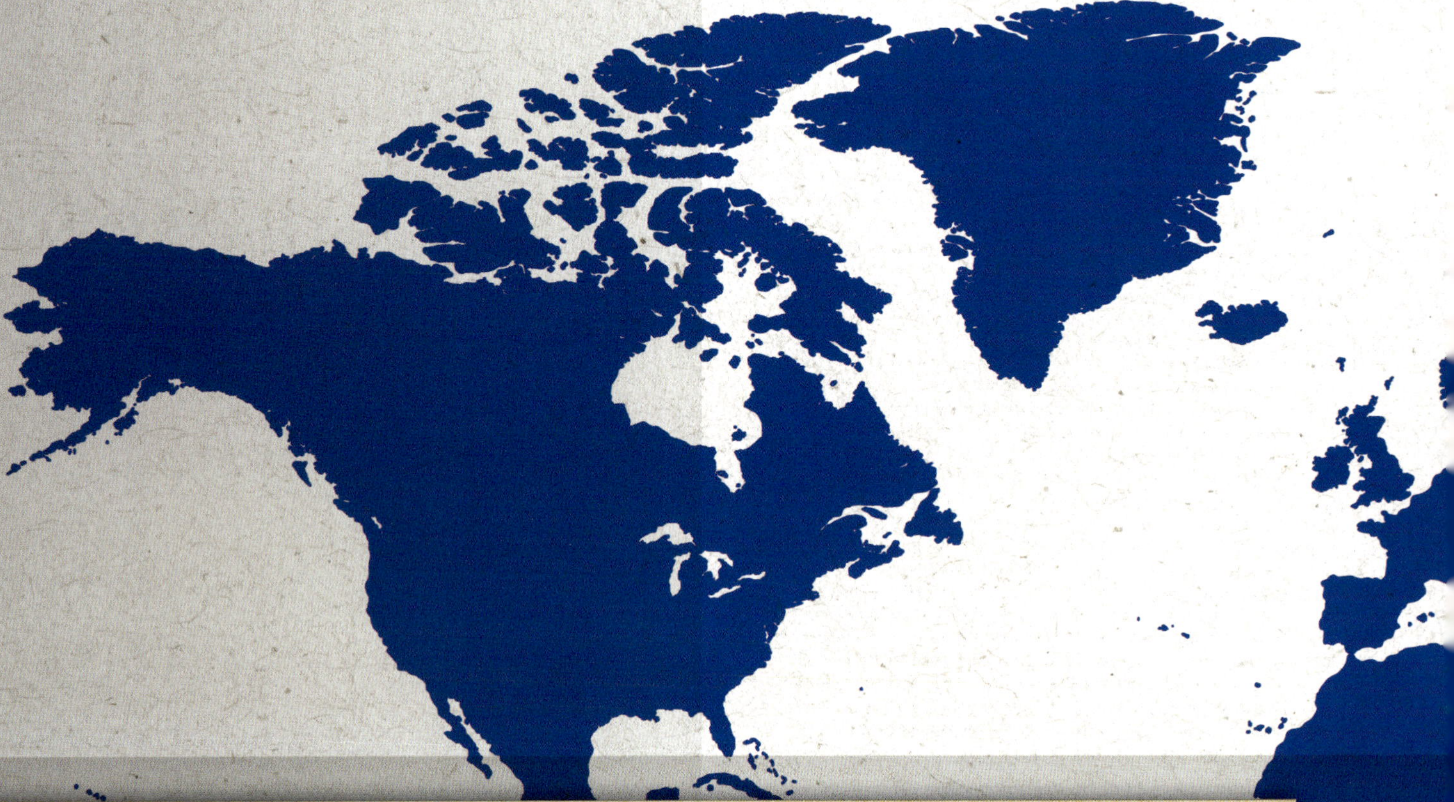

First Published 2022 by
Redback Publishing
PO Box 357 Frenchs Forest NSW 2086
Australia

www.redbackpublishing.com
orders@redbackpublishing.com

ISBN 978-1-922322-36-4

Author: Jane Hinchey
Editor: Marlene Vaughan
Design: Redback Publishing

Original illustrations © Redback Publishing 2022
Originated by Redback Publishing

Printed and bound in Malaysia

Acknowledgements
Abbreviations: l—left, r—right, b—bottom, t—top, c—centre, m—middle
We would like to thank the following for permission to reproduce
photographs: (Images © shutterstock) p9b Original Sketches, Drawings, Maps etc Collected by Admiral Isaac Smith
/Mitchell Library, State Library of New South Wales, p11br National Science Foundation, p13tl Gabriel Nerf/National Science Foundation, p13tr Natata/Shutterstock, p13br Elaine Hood/ National Science Foundation, p15tr National Science Foundation, p16tr By Administración Nacional de la Seguridad Social from Argentina via Wikipedia, p16bl Colin Whitmore/National Science Foundation, p17 mr and ml Peter Rejcek/National Science Foundation, p17br Emily Stone/National Science Foundation, p18tr Bob DeValentino/National Science Foundation, p19tr Nicki Klein/National Science Foundation, p19ml polarman/Shutterstock, p19br Melanie Conner/National Science Foundation, p20mr Michael Carroll and Rosaly Lopes/National Science Foundation, p20ml Peter Rejcek/National Science Foundation, p21br Galen Dossin/National Science Foundation, p22ml Mike Embree/National Science Foundation, p23 Lora Koenig/ National Science Foundation, p23bl Peter Rejcek/National Science Foundation, p28tl Marco Ramerini/Shutterstock, p28bl Eleanor Scriven/Shutterstock, p31br Cynthia Spence/National Science Foundation.

A catalogue record for this book is available from the National Library of Australia

CONTENTS

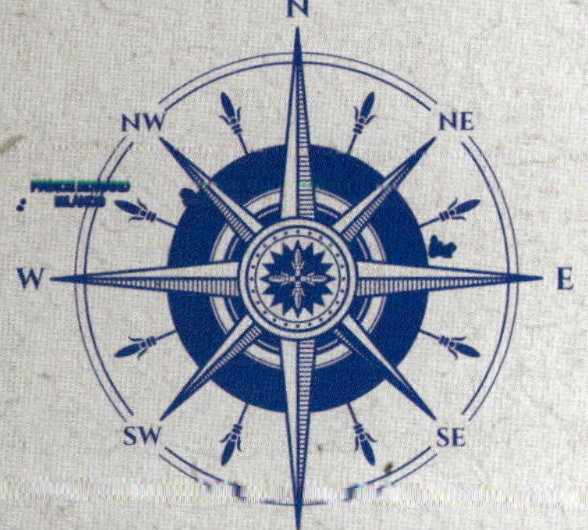

MAP OF ANTARCTICA

Countries With Antarctic Research Stations:

- Argentina
- Australia
- Belgium
- Brazil
- Bulgaria
- Chile
- China
- Czech Republic
- Ecuador
- Finland
- France
- Germany
- India
- Italy
- Japan
- New Zealand
- Norway
- Pakistan
- Peru
- Poland
- Romania
- Russia
- South Africa
- South Korea
- Spain
- Sweden
- Ukraine
- United Kingdom
- United States
- Uruguay

Antarctica

SOUTH POLE

WELCOME TO ANTARCTICA

Antarctica is the coldest, driest and windiest continent on Earth. It was once covered in forest and inhabited by many species of animals including dinosaurs. Now 98 per cent of the continent is covered by ice with no tundra, trees or bushes. There are also permanently ice-free areas that cover about one per cent of the continent. This is the subantarctic region, immediately north of the Antarctic region.

Unique blue ice cave in Antarctica

Antarctica is Earth's only continent without a native human population. The majority of Antarctica is claimed by one or more countries, although these claims are not officially recognised. In 1961 the Antarctic Treaty came into force, between 12 countries: Argentina, Australia, Belgium, Chile, France, Japan, New Zealand, Norway, South Africa, the Soviet Union, the United Kingdom and the USA.

Between them, these countries had already established over 50 Antarctic stations. The treaty now has 53 parties.

Fun Fact

Antarctica is the largest desert in the world.

DISCOVERY

Around 180 million years ago Antarctica, along with Australia, New Zealand, India, South America and South Africa was a part of the supercontinent Gondwana. Over many millions of years it broke up into the various different land masses. Around 140 million years ago, Antarctica separated and began to drift southwards.

The ancient Greeks believed there was a landmass in that region that they called Antarktikos.

It was many centuries later, between 1772 to 1775, that James Cook became the first person to navigate across the Antarctic Circle.

AT A GLANCE

Government

Antarctica does not have its own government, nor does it belong to one country, although there are numerous historical claims pending. Governance is carried out by 29 consultative nations at an annual Antarctic Treaty Consultative Meeting.

Each of the consultative nations has one or more base on the continent. Each Antarctic base is governed by the national laws of its home country.

Flag of Antarctica

Antarctica has no official flag, but Evan Townsend's 2018 design is used by many National Antarctic Programs, scientists and global activists. The flag uses the long, 3:5 format to protect the central emblem from damage by polar winds and its high contrast design allows maximum visibility in blizzards or dark polar nights. The white stripe represents long summer days and the blue, long winter nights. The central diamond shows a south-pointing compass below a snowy mountain. The flag was designed on Antarctica and first sewn from scrap tents and field bags.

Territorial Flags

Countries with research bases on the continent also fly their own national flags, or modified versions of their national flags

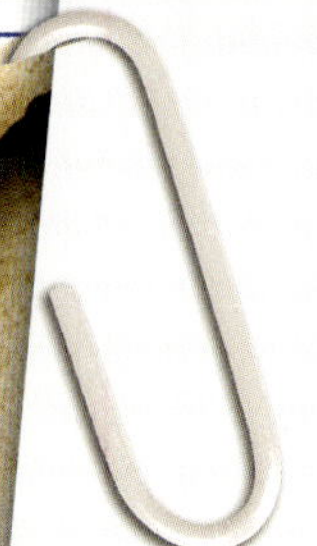

INTERNATIONAL TREATIES

Antarctic Treaty

July 1957 to December 1958 was known as International Geophysical Year. At that time there were 12 countries active in Antarctica - Argentina, Australia, Belgium, Chile, France, Japan, New Zealand, Norway, South Africa, the USSR, the United Kingdom and the United States of America. These countries were invited by the USA to a conference where a treaty was signed to 'ensure, in the interests of all mankind, that Antarctica shall continue forever to be used exclusively for peaceful purposes and shall not become the scene or object of international discord.'

These original 12 nations were later joined by Brazil, Bulgaria, the People's Republic of China, Czech Republic, Ecuador, Finland, Germany, India, Italy, South Korea, Netherlands, Peru, Poland, Spain, Sweden, the Ukraine and Uruguay to form the Consultative Parties. There are also 24 Non-Consultative Parties who are signatories to the treaty.

The treaty is a short document focussing on peace, cooperation, free exchange of scientific results, territorial sovereignty, preventing new claims, setting aside arguments over the existing ones and a ban on nuclear explosions and the dumping or radioactive waste in the region.

The Antarctic Treaty came into effect in 1961, dedicating the continent to peaceful scientific investigation. All territorial claims were suspended.

53 countries have now signed the treaty, which has resulted in Antarctica being a peaceful place.

Madrid Protocol

In 1991, the parties of the Antarctic Treaty came together to sign the Madrid Protocol, which is the framework for protecting the Antarctic environment. This designates Antarctica as a natural reserve, devoted to peace and science and requires that care for the environment is a fundamental consideration in all activities.

The Committee for Environmental Protection (CEP) was established under the Madrid Protocol, comprising of members from all the countries that are party to the protocol.

The CEP currently:

- prevents the introduction of non-native species to Antarctica
- manages the environmental implications of climatc change
- addresses how Antarctic tourism affects the environment
- addresses environmental challenges from activities conducted before the Madrid Protocol entered into force, including the clean-up of past waste disposal sites and abandoned facilities
- designate the areas of Antarctica that need special protection

Abandoned wooden huts at a whaling station

DECEPTION ISLAND

HISTORICAL CLAIMS

Seven countries have laid claim to parts of Antarctica, but any conflict for sovereignty, and any new claims cannot occur while The Antarctic Treaty is in force.

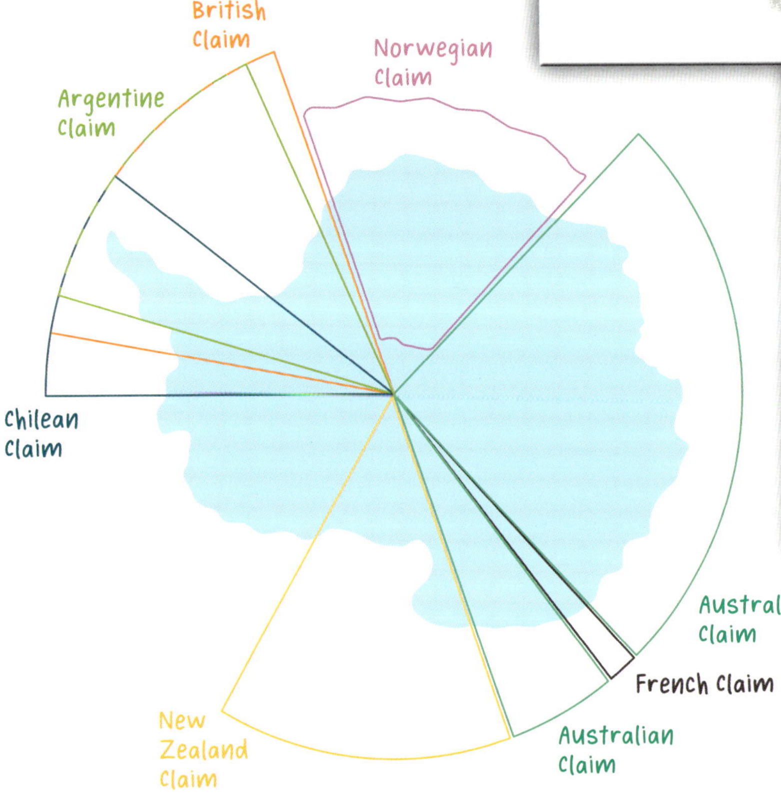

The seven historical claims to parts of Antarctica, some overlapping, are:

- Argentina
- Australia
- Chile
- France
- New Zealand
- Norway
- United Kingdom

Among the original signatories of the Antarctic Treaty were the seven countries with territorial claims. Most Treaty Parties do not recognise the territorial claims made by these seven countries and others maintain they reserve the right to make a claim.

CLOTHING AND FOOD

Buildings at the research stations are heated so the residents can wear normal clothes such as jeans and t-shirts. Outdoor clothing depends on what season it is, but generally includes insulating layers such as long woollen underwear, trousers and a shirt, and outer layers that are windproof and waterproof. Gloves and headgear are essential outside. It's important not to get so hot that you sweat, because the moisture created can cause your clothes to freeze. There is a clothing store at each station.

Meals are prepared by qualified chefs in commercial style kitchens. Food is stored carefully to maintain freshness between supply ships. Station meals are similar to what people eat at home. While there might not be as much fresh produce available, and any fresh food has spent weeks on a ship, most stations houses hydroponics facilities that ensure a steady supply of herbs, fruits and vegetables. Snacks, sweets and nuts are also supplied.

Antarctic Veggie Gardens

Crops grown at many stations include: Cucumbers, zucchinis, spinach, tomatoes, lettuces, capsicums, beans, snow peas, fennel, coriander and basil.

TIMELINE

200 Million years ago

Antarctica, Australia, and New Zealand are still a part of the supercontinent Gondwana.

45 Million years ago

Gondwana has broken up and Antarctica is now in its current position.

1772 to 1775

James Cook becomes the first person to navigate across the Antarctic Circle.

1800s

Much of the early exploration was about finding good hunting grounds for seals. In the 1890s Norwegian and Scottish expeditions explored the area for whaling.

1819 - 1820

James Bransfield sighted the Antarctic Peninsula.

Early 1900s

Many countries sent exploring expeditions to the Antarctic. The Norwegian explorer Roald Amundsen was the first to reach the South Pole on 14 December, 1911.

1907 to 1909

Ernest H. Shackleton and his team, which included legendary Australian explorer, Douglas Mawson, carried out extensive research work.

1911 to 1914

The Australasian Antarctic Expedition (AAE) with Mawson, set up huts and bases, and established the first radio communications in Antarctica.

Mid 1900s

Explorers from many countries visited Antarctica during the early half of the century. In 1957, Antarctic exploration and scientific studies became the focus of International Geophysical Year (IGY).

Mawson Station, Antarctica

1954

Australia established Mawson, its first permanent station on the Antarctic continent.

1961

IGY led to the establishment of the Antarctic Treaty, which has been signed by 53 countries. It also promotes peace and international scientific cooperation on the continent.

1998

The Madrid Protocol comes into force, designating Antarctica as a natural reserve devoted to peace and science and prohibiting mining in Antarctica.

PEOPLE AND DAILY LIFE

Research station, Antarctica

Antarctica does not have cities or any towns as we know them. It does not have an indigenous or permanent population. Anyone who lives there does so because they work on scientific research stations or bases.

Deep sea diver diving under the ice

Spread across the continent are about 70 research stations. The 29 countries that signed the Antarctic Treaty are allowed to maintain a seasonal or year-round station in Antarctica. There are about 4,000 people working in Antarctica through the summer months and about 1,000 over winter each year. Some are scientists and researchers, but there are also others who work in trades and support roles.

Some support roles include:

- Electricians
- Plumbers
- Carpenters
- Chefs
- Doctors

Working in Antarctica is not like most jobs. People don't commute there, or even fly in and out on short contracts. Contracts range from six months over the summer months, to up to a couple of years.

Paleoichnologist and mountaineer collecting trace fossils for analyses

Despite the isolation, many people see working in Antarctica as a dream job; a once in a lifetime opportunity.

THE STATIONS

There are currently 70 permanent research stations on Antarctica, representing 29 countries that are all signatories of the Antarctic Treaty. These stations are home to many people living in otherwise harsh and isolated conditions, so the living quarters and facilities are comfortable. Each expeditioner usually has his or her own room, although over the busier summer period, some people have to share. There are communal sitting areas and a dining hall, as well as laundry facilities.

Children, adolescents and teachers of the school at Esperanza Base

The Amundsen-Scott South Pole Station has lodging for 140 people, offices, a cafeteria and a gymnasium

The largest base is Amundsen-Scott South Pole Station, belonging to the United States. Australia has four stations: Casey, Mawson, Davis and Macquarie Island.

Children on Antarctica

Esperanza is an Argentinian base built in 1951. Silvia Morello de Palma, the wife of the station leader, was flown in when she was seven months pregnant. She gave birth to the first native-born Antarctican on January 7, 1978. Over the next five years, four more boys and three girls were born there. Today, around 20 children live with their families at Esperanza, with its family atmosphere and facilities making it more like a village than a scientific station.

Fast Fact

The most populous Antarctic centre is McMurdo Station on Ross Island, operated by the United States.

While each station differs, some of the facilities at the stations might include:

- A ski loop nearby
- Some outdoor sporting areas
- A cinema
- A hydroponic garden
- A medical centre
- Table tennis and pool tables
- A library
- A store

- A gym and cardio room
- A climbing wall
- A brewery and a bar

- A sauna
- A spa
- Hobby huts to use for arts and crafts
- Musical instruments and facilities for a band and performances

GETTING INVOLVED

While everyone on an Antarctic station has a job, they are also expected to participate in station duties. These duties include housekeeping and general maintenance and are allocated on a rotating roster.

As well as general duties there are many volunteer roles available, to encourage residents to be more involved in the station community.

Glacier Search and Rescue efforts are routinely practiced by Palmer Station personnel

Volunteer station positions may include roles such as:

- Firefighters and theatre nurses
- Officers in charge of flags, work, health and safety, and the gym
- Coordinators for station news, hydroponics, search and rescue, and IT
- Roles such as librarian, postal agent and hairdresser are also volunteer positions

SPORTS

Antarctica and sports don't immediately seem compatible, however the residents of this harsh continent are generally sports conscious. All the stations contain gyms, and often climbing walls and cardio rooms. A diverse range of classes such as yoga, basketball and fencing keep the expeditionists fit in winter. During the milder summer months, an array of outdoor sporting activities begin, from skiing and hiking to team sports such as rugby, soccer and softball.

Volleyball in Antarctica

Since 2006 the Antarctic Ice Marathon and 100K Ultra-marathon, have been held on Antarctica, with competitors from all over the world. The 100-kilometre race is run across a stretch of ice near the South Pole. This event hosts a few dozen cold weather loving runners from countries across the globe.

Transport

There are a number of different modes of transport at the stations, including cranes, loaders and machinery to help lift supplies from boats. Field support vehicles include snow mobiles, sleds and all terrain carriers. Expeditioners using any of the station vehicles must first undergo basic training in emergency procedures and how to drive in the given conditions.

GEOGRAPHY

Antarctica is made up of one major landmass and a number of smaller islands. It is surrounded by the Southern Ocean. About 98 per cent of the continent is covered by an ice sheet which in some areas, is over four kilometres deep. Under the ice are mountains, valleys and plains. In 2017, massive landforms were found under the ice, including three canyons, larger than the Grand Canyon. There are more than 400 known lakes, including Lake Vostok, the world's sixth largest lake. Mount Erebus, which is 3,794 meters in height, is an active volcano located in East Antarctica, on the edge of the Ross Ice Shelf.

ANTARCTICA

South Pole

Lake Vostok

Mount Erebus - 3794 metres high

Fumaroles created by gas and steam escaping from vents on Mount Erebus

Young elephant seal on South Georgia Island, Antarctica

Ice Free

When you think of Antarctica, you probably picture ice and glaciers, and you would be mainly right. Yet most Antarctic animals live in the permanently ice-free areas that cover about one per cent of the continent. This is the subantarctic region.

The Southern Ocean

The Southern Ocean surrounds the mainland of Antarctica. It is home to whales, seals and fish. Birds such as penguins and albatross all live in, or rely on these waters. Antarctic ice fish have an antifreeze protein that keeps their blood flowing.

Icebergs

Icebergs are enormous bodies of ice that break off glaciers or ice shelves. Even the small ones weigh hundreds of tonnes and they can be dangerous to ships.

Pack Ice

The Southern Ocean will often have ice floating in it. Close to the mainland are huge floating pieces of sea ice, called pack ice. It forms during the winter, more than doubling the size of the Antarctic continent, and then melts in the spring and summer. It is not attached to a shoreline and can be moved by the wind and ocean currents. Climate change impacts pack ice and the animals that live and feed around it.

Ice Shelves

Ice shelves are permanent shelves of floating ice. The Ross Ice Shelf is Antarctica's largest ice shelf and covers an area of half a million square kilometres that is about 800 kilometres across.

The Commonwealth Glacier flows through a mountain pass down into Taylor Valley

Glaciers

Glaciers are slow moving rivers of ice, formed over time from layers of compressed snow. There are many glaciers in Antarctica, including the world's largest. Lambert glacier is more than 96 kilometres wide at one point and 435 kilometres long.

Climate

Antarctica is the coldest, windiest, and driest continent on Earth. The average winter temperature from March to September is -60° Celcius, while the average summer temperature from October to February is -31° Celcius. The record low temperature in Antarctica is -89.6° Celcius.

Islands

Alexander Island

Antarctica

There are many small islands in the region. Some are ice free, while others are covered in glaciers. Alexander Island is Antarctica's largest island.

Very few of the islands are inhabited. Early landings on many islands were due to sealing in the area, but more recently visits to islands have been for research and scientific purposes.

Alexander Island - 390km long

Shore parties consist of scientists and some support crew who set up camps for anything from a few weeks to a few months. Research in the area focuses on climate change and the impact on the biodiversity and ecosystems of each island.

Research disciplines include:

- terrestrial and marine ecology
- cultural and heritage study
- geology
- vulcanology
- ecology
- glaciology
- geomorphology
- meteorology
- oceanography

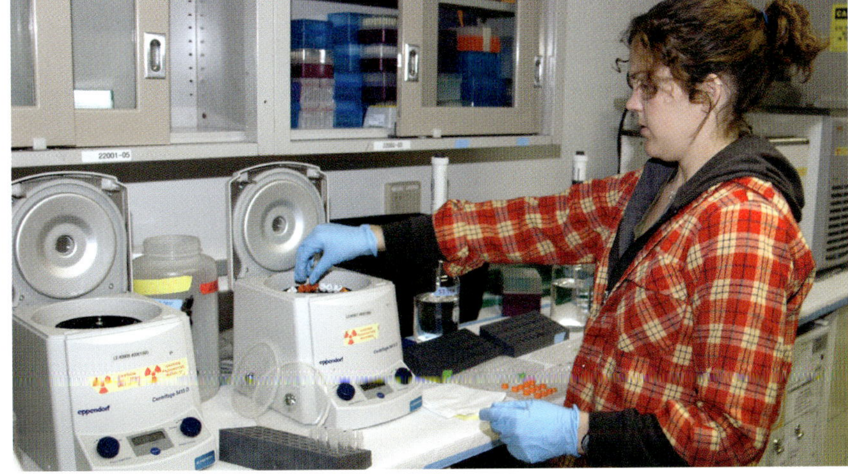

WILDLIFE

Antarctica is home to a wide range of penguins, whales, seals, krill, land invertebrates and seabirds such as albatross and terns.

Adapting to the Cold

Antarctic animals survive its freezing conditions by reducing the amount of body heat they lose. This can be through behaviours, such as huddling together like the emperor penguins, or by physical means that have evolved over time. **Some of these physical adaptations include:**

- Thick waterproof and windproof coats – Many Antarctic animals such as emperor penguins have coats that protect them from freezing water and wind.

- Extremities such as bills and flippers are smaller, meaning less blood is needed for these areas, and therefore less heat is lost.

- A thick layer of fat – Whales, seals and some penguins have layers of blubber that insulate them from the freezing conditions. Male elephant seals can use their blubber as an energy reserve and live off their fat reserves during summer.

Did You Know?

There are no fully terrestrial amphibians, mammals or reptiles in Antarctica.

Brown Skua bird stealing penguin egg

Penguins

There are 18 species of penguins and all are restricted to the Southern Hemisphere, with most on the Antarctic coasts and subantarctic islands.

Penguins feed on small fish and krill, catching these one at a time. They are also food themselves, for animals such as killer whales and leopard seals. On land, carnivorous birds steal their eggs and chicks.

Endangered, Threatened and Vulnerable

Many species of animals that live and breed in Antarctica are now under threat, due to global warming, marine pollution, invasive species, as well as increased fishing and tourism. The list of those threatened includes various breeds of whales, albatrosses and penguins.

Fast Fact

Around 88 per cent of species in the Southern Ocean are not found anywhere else in the world.

Albatross and Other Birds

Antarctica and the subantarctic islands are home to a wide range of seabirds, including petrels, terns, gulls, albatrosses, shearwaters, cormorants, gannets and boobies.

There are 22 species of albatross, and 21 of these species occur in the Southern Hemisphere. Four areas within Australian waters have been listed as critical habitat for the albatross. All species of albatross only lay a single egg. This, and the threats to their environment put the albatross at risk.

The wandering albatross is the largest of seabirds, with a wing-span reaching three metres. It can stay at sea for up to a month in search of fish and squid, often covering in excess of 10,000 kilometres on its journey.

Whales

Many species of whales are found in Antarctica. The blue whale is the largest of all whales and the largest animal to ever live on Earth. They migrate between their Antarctic summer feeding grounds and their winter breeding grounds at lower latitudes and travel long distances to find the amount of krill (their sole source of food) that they need for survival. Blue whales are blue to blue-grey in colour and grow to around 30 metres in length. They weigh about 200 tonnes and are listed as critically endangered.

Other whales found in the region include:

- Southern right whale
- Sei whale
- Fin whale
- Humpback whale

Humpback whale at feeding time

The Importance of Krill

The Antarctic ecosystem relies on krill. This tiny shrimp-like organism is the key prey species for many creatures, including fish, seals, seabirds and whales. Blue whales can eat up to four tonnes of krill per day.

TOURISM

Visitors are flocking to Antarctica. To reduce the impact of this growing trend, annual numbers are capped. In 2018-2019, there were 55,489 visitors.

A trip to Antarctica is expensive, so it is a once-in-a-lifetime adventure for many who visit. The spectacular, pristine landscapes and an abundance of incredible wildlife, often unafraid of humans, make this a very worthwhile journey.

Getting There

While some people fly, most people arrive by ship. The cruises leave from Ushuaia, located on the southernmost tip of Argentina, and South America. The shorter cruises take about 12 days, travelling through the Drake Passage to the Antarctic Peninsula and back. Some cruises are longer and incorporate activities such as mountaineering and camping. Most cruise passengers have the opportunity to experience wildlife up-close with shore excursions and activities such as kayaking.

While departures from South America are more common, it is possible to cruise from Invercargill in New Zealand and Hobart in Tasmania, Australia. These cruises take about 21 days.

There are a number of major issues impacting Antarctica.

THREATS TO ANTARCTICA

Climate Change

Climate change is the greatest threat to Antarctica. Temperatures on Antarctica's west coast have risen by three degrees Celsius since the mid-20th Century. Global warming and a rise in sea temperatures will impact land and sea ice. Already, some huge shelves of ice have collapsed and glaciers have diminished in size. Rising sea temperatures will also affect microscopic plankton, resulting in changes to the whole ocean ecosystem.

Global warming is driving polar bears toward extinction fast

Changing Ecosystems

An animal's survival often depends on the animal's ecosystem maintaining balance. Any change to the ecosystem can impact the species living there.

Plastics in Antarctica

Most litter takes hundreds of years to break down, during which time it continues to pollute the ocean and damage marine life. Items such as plastic bags or discarded fishing nets can entangle or get eaten by animals, including fish, marine birds, dolphins, whales, and seals.

Up to 12.7 million tonnes of plastic waste is washed into the world's oceans each year. These plastics are wreaking havoc with marine animals. Ocean currents can shift dangerous pollution hundreds of kilometres from its original source. For a long time scientists thought that Antarctic waters remained plastic free, however recent research shows that the Southern Ocean is also contaminated by plastics.

Human Interference

People have been visiting Antarctica for over 100 years. Although there are now treaties in place that provide strict guidelines on what activities can take place there and how to treat the environment, this wasn't always the case. Early exploration teams left their mark on the formerly pristine environment. After the signing of the Antarctic Treaty, countries were responsible for cleaning up human waste; however each country did this in different ways. Some removed the waste from the continent, others simply buried it.

Excess materials and waste are stored outside ready for removal

Tourism – The Last Frontier

Tourism to Antarctica is rising rapidly. To reduce the impact of this growing trend, annual numbers are capped.

Overfishing

While the Southern Ocean experiences less fishing than other oceans, due to expense and dangerous sea conditions, it is still overfished. Nowadays, fishing boats must have a license, which sets a specific area and time period to fish and as well as restricting the species and size of catch that is allowed.

GLOSSARY

Antarctic Treaty international treaty that made Antarctica a place for peaceful, scientific research

Blue whale largest creature on earth

Cook, Captain James first person to cross the Antarctic Circle

critical at a turning point for survival

ecosystem living and non-living parts of an area and the interactions between them

endangered may soon become extinct

endemic only found in a certain place

extinct no longer in existence

feral predators non-native animals that kill and eat other animals

glacier river of ice

habitat place where plants and animals live

icebergs huge pieces of floating ice

ice cliff walls of ice where glaciers meet the sea

pack ice floating pieces of sea ice

recovery plan plan for the conservation of a species

species one kind of living thing

territorial claims when a country claims it owns part of Antarctica

threat anything that may reduce the numbers of a species

threatened endangered or vulnerable

vulnerable may soon become endangered

INDEX

ARCTIC OCEAN
GREENLAND
(DENMARK)
ALASKA (USA)
CANADA
ICELAND
FAROE ISLANDS
UNITED KINGDOM
IRELAND
FRANCE
NORTH PACIFIC OCEAN
UNITED STATES
NORTH ATLANTIC OCEAN
PORTUGAL
SPAIN
MOROCCO
ALGERIA
CANARY ISLANDS
(SPAIN)
MEXICO
THE BAHAMAS
CUBA
HAITI
JAMAICA
BELIZE
GUATEMALA
HONDURAS
EL SALVADOR
NICARAGUA
COSTA RICA
PANAMA
CAPE VERDE
MAURITANIA
MALI
SENEGAL
BURKINA FASO
THE GAMBIA
GUINEA-BISSAU
GUINEA
COTE D'IVOIRE
GHANA
SIERRA LEONE
LIBERIA
VENEZUELA
GUYANA
SURINAME
FRENCH GUIANA
COLOMBIA
LINES ISLANDS
ECUADOR
PERU
BRAZIL
COOK ISLANDS
SOUTH PACIFIC OCEAN
BOLIVIA
FRENCH POLYNESIA
PARAGUAY
SOUTH ATLANTIC OCEAN
ST.HELENA
EASTER ISLAND
URUGUAY
ARGENTINA
CHILE
TRISTAN DA CUNHA
GOUGH ISLAND
FALKLAND ISLANDS (UK)
SOUTH GEORGIA (UK)